The Battle of Britain for Kids

The English Reading Tree

Keith Goodman

Published by G-L-R (Great Little Read)

Copyright: The English Reading Tree/GLR

This book is sold subject to the condition that it shall not by way of trade or otherwise be resold or hired out or otherwise circulated without the written or verbal consent of the author.

Written by Keith Goodman

Reading Age for this book: 8+

The reading age for the series will vary but starts at seven

The English Reading Tree Series has been written for children aged seven and over. It is the perfect tool for parents to get their children into the habit of reading.

This book has been created to entertain and educate young minds and is packed with information, trivia, and lots of authentic images that bring the topic alive.

There is a quiz at the end to test how much has been learned

TABLE OF CONTENTS

Introduction 5

Timeline Battle of Britain 7

Dunkirk 9

Operation Dynamo 11

The First Phase of Battle of Britain 13

The Battle Begins 14

Radar and the Battle of Britain 16

Phase Two of the Battle of Britain 19

Eagle Day 20

The Hardest Day 23

Phase Three of the Battle of Britain 25

The Luftwaffe Attacks London 26

Phase Four of the Battle of Britain 29

Battle of Britain Day 31

Reasons why Germany lost the Battle of Britain 34

The Blitz 37

Coventry 41

The Battle of Britain Planes...43

Hermann Goering 52

Air Chief Marshal Hugh Dowding 54

Battle of Britain Quiz 56

Thank you for Reading this Book..57

Battle of Britain Quiz Answers 62

Attributions 63

Introduction

The Battle of Britain was a unique historic occurrence.

It was the first time a large-scale military campaign had been fought solely by planes and it almost brought Britain to the brink of defeat and invasion by the German military.

Let's look at why this battle was fought above the skies of Britain and why against all odds, the British were able to grasp victory from the jaws of a devastating defeat.

Timeline Battle of Britain

The Battle of Britain Timeline starts on the 10th of July 1940 and ends on the 31st of October 1940.

The beginning of World War Two has a timeline that leads up to the Battle of Britain.

The **1st of September 1939** was the day that German troops crossed into Poland. Two days after, France and Britain declared war on Germany. This was the beginning of World War Two.

Poland fell, and Germany invaded Denmark, Norway, Belgium, Luxembourg, Holland and France.

British troops were evacuated from Dunkirk.

France fell in June 1940.

With France defeated, Germany started to make plans to invade Britain.

This could only be done if Germany could get control of British airspace.

On June the 30th, 1940, the Battle of France was over, and the Battle of Britain was about to begin.

Dunkirk

Troops waiting to be rescued on the beaches of Dunkirk

Dunkirk is a tiny coastal town in Northern France. It was the scene of one of the most incredible military evacuations ever. The Battle of Dunkirk lasted from the 26th of May 1940 to the 4th of June 1940.

During the fighting, around 338,000 British and Allied troops were rescued from the beaches and evacuated to England by boat. The German military had trapped the soldiers on the beach and expected them to surrender.

However, as German forces closed in, hundreds of British naval and civilian ships and boats traveled across the English Channel to rescue the Allied troops.

It was known as the Miracle of Dunkirk.

Operation Dynamo

Operation Dynamo was the codename for the largest evacuation ever seen.

It started on May 26, 1940.

The German air force (Luftwaffe) bombed the beaches of Dunkirk and the small harbor. This slowed the evacuation, and only 7500 soldiers could leave on the first day.

Because the beach at Dunkirk was so shallow, large Navy ships couldn't go in too close.

A call was sent out for smaller civilian ships to go across the English Channel to Dunkirk.

Around 1,200 ships and boats were eventually used. Some of them were extremely small such as leisure craft and fishing boats.

The first boats arrived on the beaches of Dunkirk on the morning of May 28.

British Prime Minister Winston Churchill only expected to rescue 45,000 troops. Operation Dynamo was so successful that by the time the rescue was over, 198,000 British and 140,000 French troops made it to England to fight another day.

German troops overran Dunkirk on June 4, 1940.

Even though the evacuation had been successful, thousands of troops had not been rescued and were taken prisoner by the Germans.

Germany now controlled mainland Europe and turned its attention to invading Britain.

The First Phase of Battle of Britain

On the **10th of July 1940**, the German Luftwaffe began attacking ships in the English Channel. The Luftwaffe also bombed English Channel ports and coastal radar stations.

On **July 6th, 1940**, the German leader, Adolph Hitler, ordered preparations begin for Operation Sealion, which was the invasion of Britain.

Hitler ordered that the British Air Force (RAF) be destroyed so it couldn't stop an invasion.

The Battle Begins

German planes over the English Channel in 1940

German bombers started their bombing attacks on Britain on July 10, 1940. This was the start of the Battle of Britain, which lasted three months.

Germany had overrun France. Even though many Allies troops had been saved from the beaches of Dunkirk, Britain stood alone and faced an invasion.

On this day, around 120 German bombers attacked a British convoy of merchant ships, and 70 more German bombers attacked the dockyards in South Wales.

The British had fewer planes than the Germans but had the advantage of radar. They also had the famous spitfire planes, which were deadly in air combat and could turn much quicker than German fighters.

German single-engine fighters didn't have the range to protect bombers and had to turn back and leave bombers unprotected.

One major problem for the British was the lack of aircraft. An appeal was made to the British public. "Give the government your pots and pans, and we will turn them into spitfires and hurricanes." People donated anything they could for the war effort.

Radar and the Battle of Britain

Radio detecting and ranging (RADAR) was essential in the success of the British air defenses against the German Air Force.

Radar could find incoming enemy aircraft approaching by bouncing sound waves off them. British radar operators could tell where the enemy planes were, how many were attacking and where they were going.

The information was sent to the air force, and planes could be sent to attack.

RADAR early warning was very effective

Radar was a crucial part of the British defense system and meant that even though the Germans had more planes, the British could use the planes that they had very efficiently.

A network of radar stations was built all over the east coast of Britain. In 1940, the system was very effective at spotting German planes, even if they were flying low.

Radar had been invented in Germany, but the German leaders didn't realize how vital it could be in the Battle of Britain.

Although some British radar stations were attacked, there was never a significant German effort to destroy British radar defenses.

Phase Two of the Battle of Britain

This period in the battle started on August 13 and ended on August 18, 1940. It consisted of the Luftwaffe attacking British airfields and radar stations along the east coast.

The German plan was simple. The Luftwaffe would destroy the Royal Air Force (RAF) either while the planes were still on the ground or when they engaged in fights in the air. The German High Command was also aware of the usefulness of radar to the British and wanted to bomb as many radar stations as possible.

The attacks on airfields were successful, and many were damaged by bombs.

On the **13th of August 1940**, the Germans launched Eagle Day, which consisted of raids on RAF airfields in the Southeast of England.

On the **18th of August 1940**, the Hardest Day saw battles in the air between the RAF and the Luftwaffe, with more attacks on airfields.

Eagle Day

German Messerschmitt BF 110s suffered heavy losses on this day

Adlertag, or Eagle Day, was the day that the German High Command planned to bring Britain to its knees and open the way for a full invasion. However, it didn't go entirely to plan.

August the 13th saw the head of the Luftwaffe, Hermann Goering, very confident that he could destroy the RAF. Up to this date, the German advance through Europe had been impressive. Invading Britain would mean crossing the English Channel; without air superiority, this would be almost impossible.

The code name for the operation was Adlerangriff (Eagle Attack). It was a failure.

On the 13th of August, the Luftwaffe launched wave after wave of bomber attacks on British airfields. The plan was simple. The RAF planes could not get into the air or land without airfields. This would leave the sky above Britain clear for the Luftwaffe to take control.

German leader Hitler was convinced that if this were achieved, the British would surrender.

The day started badly for the German bombers and fighters. The weather was terrible, and the British planes attacked them at every opportunity. German losses were very high and could have been well over fifty planes.

The RAF used the Dowding System to respond to raids. The system was in place well before the Battle of Britain. Unlike the confused German attack, the Dowding System was straightforward and easy to follow. Radar and lookouts would pick up the enemy aircraft and feed the information to a fighter control station. The fighter control station would then tell the RAF where to send planes to fight the German planes.

The German bomber attacks had little effect on the daily operation of targeted airfields. Those that were hit were operational again within twenty-four hours.

As well as airfields, there were some bomber raids on British towns and cities.

The Hardest Day

British pilots waiting to go into action

The Battle of Britain took place more than eighty years ago, and most people think the peak of the fighting happened on the 15th of September 1940. However, from German and British records, the 18th of August proved to be the 'Hardest Day.'

On this day, the Luftwaffe flew over eight hundred missions and the RAF nine hundred and twenty missions in response.

The Luftwaffe pilots were determined to destroy several vital British airfields on this day. These were at Biggin Hill, Kenley,

Gosport, Ford, Thorney Island, North Weald and Hornchurch. They also attacked a radar station at Poling.

The battles in the air were some of the biggest ever seen at the time. The British shot down more of the Luftwaffe than they lost, but many British planes were destroyed on the ground.

Both sides lost more planes that day than at any other point during the war. This includes the infamous Battle of Britain Day in September.

Phase Three of the Battle of Britain

This phase started on August 19th and went through until September 6th. During this period, the Luftwaffe continuously bombed towns, cities and airfields in the South East of England, the North East and the Midlands.

On the 20th of August 1940, the famous speech by Winston Churchill recognized how much Britain owed to the British and Allied pilots and crews. He said, "Never in the field of human conflict has so much been owed by so many to so few."

On the 24th of August, German pilots dropped bombs on London by mistake. The following day the RAF attacked Berlin in retaliation.

On the 31st of August, British plane losses were the heaviest to date

The Luftwaffe Attacks London

London docks under attack at the start of the Blitz

All through August, the Luftwaffe attacked airfields and radar stations. The situation for Britain was not good, and many planes and pilots were lost.

Germany needed to control the skies to transport troops across the 21-mile English Channel. Because of this, the attack intensified in August, and at times more than 1,500 German planes crossed over from Europe every day to bomb targets.

The RAF put up a gallant resistance, but it became clear by the end of August that this may not have been enough.

Just as the situation looked like it couldn't get any worse, the German leader, Adolph Hitler, made a terrible mistake.

The RAF had been ordered to attack the German capital city, Berlin, and Hitler was furious, as he had specifically stopped the Luftwaffe from attacking the British capital, London.

Hitler orders the Luftwaffe to stop its attacks on airfields and attack London and other British cities.

On the 7th of September 1940, the 'Blitz' began, and in a short time, London was in flames with churches, hospitals and the royal palace suffering hits. The raids were supposed to cause terror and make the civilian population want to surrender. Instead, it had the opposite effect.

The people living in the British cities became even more determined to beat Hitler and the German war machine.

These raids on London gave the RAF time to put airfields back in service, train more pilots and make more planes.

Phase Four of the Battle of Britain

The fourth and final phase of the Battle of Britain started on September 7th with the bombing of London and other cities and ended on October 31st.

The **15th of September 1940** is called Battle of Britain Day. On this day, the Luftwaffe launched its biggest raid on London. The RAF successfully fought off the attack, and German losses were very high.

On the **17th of September 1940**, the loss of planes during Battle of Britain day was enough for Hitler to cancel his invasion plan codenamed Operation Sealion.

On the **26th of September 1940**, the Luftwaffe bombed the Spitfire factory in Southampton and destroyed it.

Throughout **October 1940**, the Luftwaffe bombed important British cities during the night. Towns on the East Coast were also attacked, and some military targets during daylight hours.

By the **31st of October 1940**, it had become increasingly clear that the RAF was far from beaten. Although German planes still bombed cities, the battle of Britain was effectively finished.

Although Britain had stood alone during the Battle of Britain, many pilots fighting to defeat the Luftwaffe were from other countries. These included:

- Poland
- New Zealand
- Australia
- Canada
- Czechoslovakia
- Belgium
- France
- USA
- South Africa

Battle of Britain Day

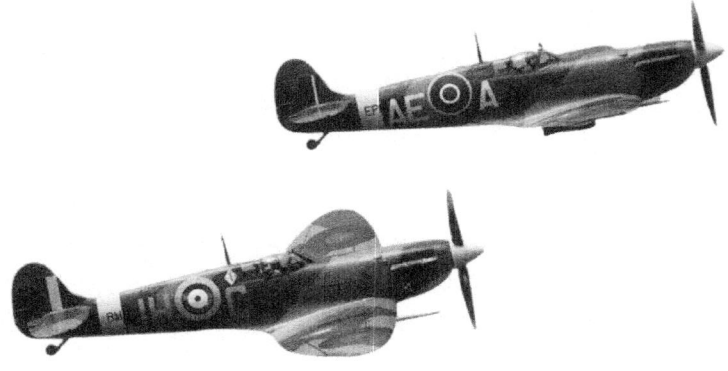

Cover picture of Two Spitfires

The day that came to be known as Battle of Britain Day occurred on the 15th of September 1940.

The Luftwaffe launched two massive waves of bombers on London, thinking the RAF was nearly defeated.

The Germans had switched tactics on the 7th of September 1940 and had begun to attack London rather than RAF bases and radar stations.

This had given the RAF pilots time to recover and new planes to be delivered. By the 15th of September, the RAF was very well prepared.

The first wave had 250 German bombers. The RAF attacked these, and only about half made it to London.

A second wave of 250 German planes arrived at 2 pm and was attacked by the RAF. By now, all of the planes that the British had were airborne. There were no planes in reserve. The fighting was fierce, and Londoners stood in the streets to watch the battles above their heads.

Many German bombers were scattered and were forced to drop their bombs in the countryside and not on London.

Although the British claimed to have shot down almost 200 German planes, the number was around 60. The RAF lost 31 planes.

The 15th of September was a massive defeat for the Germans. Although the raids continued and the Blitz on British cities would not end until the following year, the invasion was now not an option open to Adolph Hitler, the German leader.

Germany carried on bombing London at night until May 1941. At one point, London was attacked for 57 nights in a row.

When Hitler decided to invade Russia, the bombing stopped, as he needed planes for the Eastern Front.

Reasons why Germany lost the Battle of Britain

The German leader, Adolph Hitler, was over-confident. Many thought the German air force was the most formidable in the world. It was certainly the biggest. Hitler underestimated the British air defenses, and his idea that the RAF could be defeated in four days was ludicrous.

The head of the Luftwaffe was Hermann Goering, a World War One Flying Ace. However, he was not a great tactician, had out-of-date ideas about modern airpower, and often made erratic decisions. Adolph Hitler's constant meddling also hindered him.

Britain had a state-of-the-art early warning system called radar. This meant that, even though there were more German planes, the British could send their planes to where they were needed most. It also meant that the RAF could respond quickly to a German attack and be waiting for the German bombers. Britain had a chain of radar stations situated all along its East Coast. By the time Goering realized the importance of destroying the radar stations, it was too late. The stations were difficult to destroy and very easy to replace.

The planes of the RAF could stay in the sky longer because they were fighting over Britain. The German planes needed to know how much fuel was needed to get home.

If an RAF plane was shot down, the pilot could bail out and be back up in the air in another plane very quickly. A German pilot who bailed out would end up as a prisoner of war.

German intelligence consistently underestimated the number of planes that the RAF had. This meant the German bomber crews were often shocked by the number of fighters they encountered.

The change in tactics from attacking airfields to cities was crucial, and it gave the RAF time to build more planes and train more pilots.

By the end of October 1940, there had been 114 days of fighting above Britain.

Germany had lost 1,733 planes and 3,893 crew.

The RAF had lost 828 planes and 1,007 crew.

The Blitz

People sheltered in underground stations below the city of London

Living in any British city during the Second World War was extremely dangerous. This was because they became targets for the Luftwaffe. The German air force flew over British cities and dropped bombs in the hope of forcing Britain to either negotiate peace or surrender.

This period of the war became known as the Blitz, which is a shortened form of the German word Blitzkrieg. This word means lightning war.

Although by the middle of September 1940, the German leader, Adolph Hitler, had given up plans to invade Britain. The German air force continued to bomb British cities. London was the primary target.

The heavy and frequent attacks on London by the Luftwaffe continued nightly from September 1940 until May 1941. German bombers also attacked other cities, industrial areas and ports.

London was bombed every day and night (except one night) for a series of eleven weeks. By the end of this period, over a third of the city had been destroyed.

Thousands of bombs were dropped, and thousands of people lost their lives, but the blitz became part of the day-to-day life of Londoners.

Many children were evacuated to the countryside, which was much safer.

The aftermath of a German air raid

A siren warned those people that remained of an impending attack. The siren sounded again when the attack was over. People would emerge from their shelters, hoping their houses had not been destroyed.

Along with London, other cities bombed included Cardiff, Swansea, Bristol, Southampton, Liverpool, Birmingham and Plymouth.

As a result of the Blitz, over 32,000 British civilians lost their lives, and 87,000 were seriously injured.

Bombs destroyed two million buildings.

The Blitz ended in the middle of May 1941. The German air force was needed for the invasion of Russia.

Coventry

Coventry city center after the attack

On the 14th of November 1940, the English city of Coventry was targeted by German bombers. The resulting attack was so destructive that it horrified the rest of Britain and is still remembered today.

Operation Moonlight Sonata (as the German High Command called it) started in the early evening. Bombs that destroyed water supplies, gas, electricity and telephone lines were dropped.

Buildings and roads were attacked, and very soon, even the renowned ancient cathedral was on fire. A wall of flames engulfed the city.

The wave after wave of attacks peaked at midnight, but the all-clear signal didn't sound until six o'clock in the morning.

By the time the attack had finished, around 5,000 buildings had been destroyed and many factories damaged.

With 600 people killed and many more missing or injured, this was a night Coventry would never forget.

The air raid would not affect the war's outcome but would go down in history as the most concentrated attack on a British city during the Second World War.

It was said that German leader Adolph Hitler ordered the attack as revenge for the RAF attacking Munich.

The Battle of Britain Planes

The Supermarine Spitfire (British)

This is the iconic British plane of the Second World War, symbolizing the British victory in the Battle of Britain. It was speedy and shot down over 500 German planes for the loss of just 320.

20,350 Spitfires were built

The Hawker Hurricane (British)

More hurricanes were built for the Battle of Britain than any other plane. The design was wood and metal covered in fabric. This was similar to the early bi-planes of World War One.

Despite the old-style design, the Hurricane was easy to maintain and was a steady flyer and rugged fighter.

The superior Spitfire was used to fight with bomber escort planes, while the Hurricanes attacked the slower bombers.

The Hawker Hurricane

The Hurricanes shot down 565 enemy planes for the loss of 404.

14,487 Hurricanes were built

The Boulton Paul Defiant (British)

The Defiant was a British two-seater plane with a four-gun power-operated turret.

It had no forward-facing gun, so it could not attack from behind.

This plane took part in early battles during the Dunkirk evacuation and at the start of the Battle of Britain.

It was soon realized that the gun turret was an old-fashioned concept for fighter planes.

It was no match for the superior firepower of the Luftwaffe.

1,064 of these planes were built

Messerschmitt BF 109   (German)

This was a fighter plane, which was thought to be the best at the time. The Germans assumed that the British fighter planes would be no match.

The Messerschmitt could fly faster than the Spitfire at high altitudes and dive more rapidly. It also had better guns.

Also, the German pilots at the start of the Battle of Britain were battle-hardened veterans.

The Messerschmitt didn't have the range to fly far over Britain and had limited ammunition.

The Luftwaffe began the Battle of Britain with 1,100 BF 109s, but by the end, 650 had been shot down by the RAF.

32,248 were built

Messerschmitt BF 110 (German)

This was a two-seater plane that was a long-range fighter escort. Although it was fast and well-armed, it didn't have good maneuverability and was not as good as the RAF fighters.

6,000 were built.

Heinkel He 111 (German)

This was one of the main German bomber planes; however, it was slow, poorly armed and didn't carry a big bomb load. It was very durable and would often be able to fly back to base riddled with bullet holes and badly damaged.

Around 6,000 were built.

Dornier Do 17 (German)

Nicknamed the Flying Pencil, it was designed before World War Two as a high-speed mail plane. It was later converted into a bomber. It had a limited range and could not carry a big bomb load. Many were lost during the Battle of Britain.

Around 2,000 were built.

Junkers Ju 88 (German)

Inside the cockpit of a Ju 88

This was the most modern of the German bombers in 1940. The plane had been designed and built as a medium bomber that could travel at high speed. Because of some structural changes to turn it into a dive-bomber, its performance was reduced.

15,000 were built.

Junkers Ju 87 (German)

This was the famous Stuka dive-bomber that was highly successful at the beginning of the war. Because of its vertical dive and pinpoint bombing, it was triumphant in the campaigns in Poland and France. It was a different story during the Battle of Britain, and many were shot down by the RAF. On just one day, 12 were shot down, and many others were severely damaged. This meant they were gradually phased out of the battle in the skies above Britain.

The Junker 87 was easily identifiable by its inverted gullwing

6,000 were built

Hermann Goering

Goering on trial for war crimes

Goering started his military career in the German infantry in 1915. He transferred to the air service and was a very successful fighter pilot.

When Adolph Hitler came to power, Goering was made head of the Luftwaffe.

He was successful in the opening campaigns of World War two, but in The Battle of Britain, he lacked the technical skill and organization to defeat the RAF. His lack of a clear plan and Hitler's constant interference led to the defeat of the Luftwaffe.

Goering made the fatal mistake of underestimating the strength of the RAF. He also moved the focus of the attack from bombing British airfields to attacking cities. This gave the RAF time to recover and build more planes.

Failure to defeat Britain meant that Germany would be fighting a war on two fronts after the invasion of Russia.

The Americans arrested Goering in 1945. He committed suicide while in captivity.

Air Chief Marshal Hugh Dowding

Dowding was the principal architect of the British victory in the Battle of Britain.

He started his military career in 1913 and was the leader of number 16 squadron during World War One.

Dowding was in charge of RAF Fighter Command during the Battle of Britain. Because of his meticulous preparation for the attack on Britain, he has often been credited as winning the battle against the Luftwaffe, though not without criticism for his tactics.

He was removed from his post in November 1940.

He retired in 1942.

Battle of Britain Quiz

1 What year did the Battle of Britain take place?

2 What's another name for radio detecting and ranging?

3 What did the attacks on London and other British cities become known as?

4 What was the German codename for the invasion of Britain?

5 Who was head of the Luftwaffe during the Battle of Britain?

6 What is the 15th of September 1940 known as?

7 Operation Moonlight Sonata was the codename for the attack on which city?

8 What plane was nicknamed the Flying Pencil?

Thank you for Reading this Book

You can visit the English Reading Tree Page by clicking:

Visit Amazon's Keith Goodman Page (Mailing List)

Books in the English Reading Tree Series by Keith Goodman include:

The Titanic for Kids

Shark Facts for Kids

Solar System Facts for Kids

Dinosaur Facts for Kids

Save the Titanic for Kids

Discovering Ancient Egypt for Kids

Native American Culture for Kids

The American Civil War Explained for Kids

The American Revolution Explained for Kids

World War One in Brief for Kids

World War Two Explained for Kids

Middle Ages Facts and Trivia for kids

The Cold War Explained for Kids

The Great Depression and Stuff for Kids

Discovering Ancient Greece for Kids

The Vikings for Kids

The History of Ancient Weapons

Titanic Conspiracy Theories for Kids

The French Revolution Explained for Kids

The Bermuda Triangle Mystery for Kids

The Russian Revolution Explained for Kids

UFO Mysteries for Kids

Ancient Mesopotamia for Kids

Chinese Dynasties for Kids for Kids

Myths and Legends for Kids

The Loch Ness Monster for Kids

Ghost Stories for Kids

The Bigfoot Mystery for Kids

Unexplained Mysteries for Kids

The Vietnam War for Kids

The Knights Templar for Kids

The Crusades Explained for kids

The Ancient Incas for Kids

World War One Planes for Kids

The Battle of Britain for Kids

Books in the Young Learner series

All About the Anglo Saxons

All About the Titanic

All About the Battle of the Little Bighorn

All About the Second World War

All About the American Revolutionary War

All About American History

All About George Washington

All About the Normans

All About Japan

All About Stonehenge

All About Castles

All About the Hundred Years' War

All About World War Two Tanks

All About Queen Elizabeth II

Living History Series

1 Ancient Britain for Kids

2 Roman Britain for kids

3 Anglo-Saxon Britain for Kids

4 Viking Britain for Kids

5 Norman Britain for Kids

6 Plantagenet England for Kids

7 Tudor England for Kids

8 17th Century England for Kids

9 Georgian Britain for Kids

10 Victorian Britain for Kids

11 Britain at War for Kids

12 World War Two Britain for Kids

Battle of Britain Quiz Answers

1 1940

2 RADAR

3 The Blitz

4 Operation Sealion

5 Hermann Goering

6 The Battle of Britain Day

7 Coventry

8 Dornier Do 17

Attributions

Bundesarchiv, Bild 141-0678 / CC-BY-SA 3.0, CC BY-SA 3.0 DE <https://creativecommons.org/licenses/by-sa/3.0/de/deed.en>, via Wikimedia Commons

Find the author of this image here: https://commons.wikimedia.org/wiki/File:Bundesarchiv_Bild_141-0678,_Flugzeuge_Heinkel_He_111.jpg

Bundesarchiv, Bild 101I-427-0412-033 / Lempp / CC-BY-SA 3.0, CC BY-SA 3.0 DE <https://creativecommons.org/licenses/by-sa/3.0/de/deed.en>, via Wikimedia Commons

Flugzeug Messerschmitt Me

Find the author of this image here: https://commons.wikimedia.org/wiki/File:Bundesarchiv_Bild_101I-427-0412-033,_Flugzeug_Messerschmitt_Me_110.jpg

FOTO:FORTEPAN /Szabó Barbara, CC BY-SA 3.0 <https://creativecommons.org/licenses/by-sa/3.0>, via Wikimedia Commons

HE 111

Find the author of this image here:

https://commons.wikimedia.org/wiki/File:HE_111_fortepan_116526.jpg

Bundesarchiv, Bild 101I-342-0603-25 / Ketelhohn [Kettelhohn] / CC-BY-SA 3.0, CC BY-SA 3.0 DE <https://creativecommons.org/licenses/by-sa/3.0/de/deed.en>, via Wikimedia Commons

Dornier Do 17

Find the author of this image here:

https://commons.wikimedia.org/wiki/File:Bundesarchiv_Bild_101I-342-0603-25,_Belgien-Frankreich,_Flugzeuge_Dornier_Do_17.jpg

Printed in Great Britain
by Amazon